I0748452

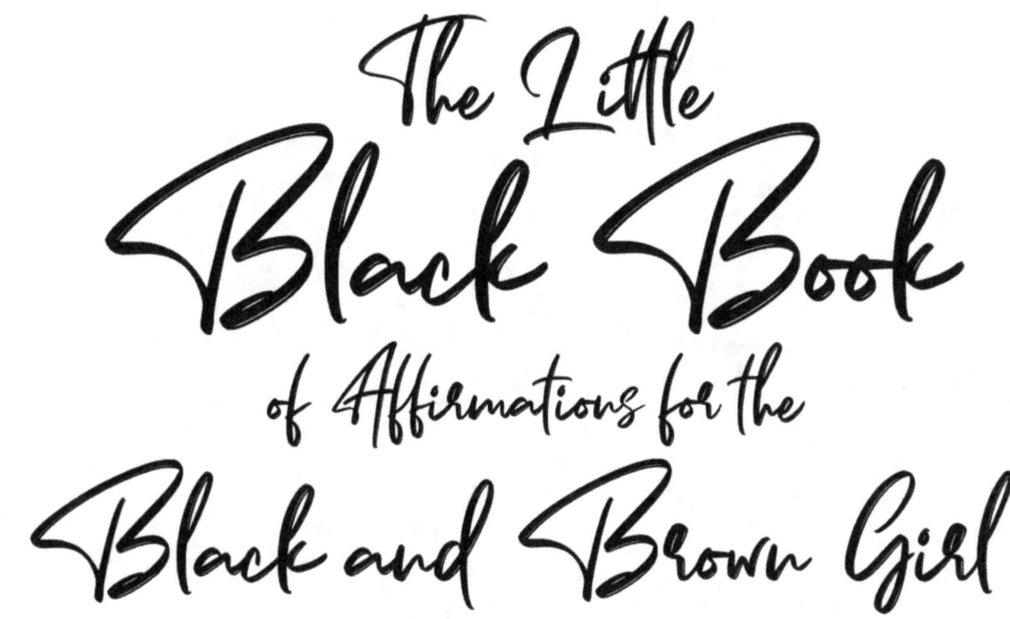

A 52-Week Guide
for Loving Yourself, Others, and The Life You Live

Hardcover ISBN: 978-1-63616-090-0
Ebook ISBN: 978-1-63616-091-7

Published By Opportune Independent Publishing Co.
www. opportunepublishing.com

Printed in the United States of America

About the Author

Dr. Ashley A. Nazon, DSW, LCSW, QS was born and raised in Chicago, IL. Dr. Nazon has always had a passion for helping others since childhood. It is with that passion that she chose a lifetime of servitude helping others overcome personal and professional obstacles.

Dr. Nazon graduated from the illustrious Florida A&M University (FAMU as the true rattlers call it) in 2010 with a Bachelor of Social Work (BSW) degree. Upon successfully earning her BSW, Dr. Nazon went on to earn her Master of Social Work degree from the University of Central Florida in 2013 before courageously taking the steps to earn the Doctorate in Social Work from Capella University in 2019.

Dr. Nazon has numerous years of experience providing therapeutic and case management services. Currently, Dr. Nazon owns a private practice in Tampa, FL where her mission is to help clients re-discover a zeal for their lives, careers, families, and most importantly a love for self. Dr. Nazon's favorite mantra is "Holistic Health Leads to A Healthier Living."

Introduction

As women we go through life being told that we have to be strong and at times even struggle to feel as if we deserve the goodness in the world. I am here to tell you that we all deserve goodness in every aspect of our lives without having to be strong or self-sacrifice. We need to consistently remind ourselves of how wonderful we are without all the noise of the outside world. Love yourself enough to defy your own odds and self-imposed limits. Greatness, gratitude, and love are awaiting you. Are you ready?

I cannot wait for you to start using this guide, but before you do let us focus on clearing our minds and hearts. Before you do the weekly affirmations, mindfulness practice, or set your intentions be sure to take 5- 10 minutes to do 3 deep breaths. Each deep breathe should be held for 10 seconds (if you can) and then release slowly. Now dive in!

As we move through the year we are constantly shedding and growing into the most beautiful versions of ourselves.

Sending You Love & Light!

Terms and concepts used in this book:

When you see "I am" statements these are positive affirmations to use the week it is assigned.

Mindfulness moments — Mindfulness practice encourages us to take a moment and reflect on our thoughts and feelings and analyze why we feel or think certain thoughts. Mindfulness moments will be cued when asked directly about your feelings for the week.

Intentions — Purposeful thoughts or actions that should be completed throughout the week.

“New year, New You,” As They Say

January

Week 1

I am the sh**and my ancestors have my back daily! I am beautiful, loved, and cared for.

For Your Thoughts

Week 2

Everyone and everything works for my greater good in this beautiful universe.

For Your Thoughts

Week 3

3rd week of the month, how are you feeling girl??
Self-check, how is your month going? Are you still feeling fabulous?
You are black/brown girl magic!

For Your Thoughts

Week 4

We made it! It's the end of the month! What did we accomplish? Did you show up this month how you wanted? The self-love doesn't stop... we are moving into another month - How do we want to show up for the next 30 days?

For Your Thoughts

It's All About Love

Things to say to yourself this month

February

Week 1

Thank you ancestors for your continued abundance of love and protection- I am the vision of my ancestors!

For Your Thoughts

Week 2

I love you- thank you body, mind, and spirit for your continued support during this month.

For Your Thoughts

Week 3

My happiness continues to radiate and attracts an abundance of love in all areas of my life.

For Your Thoughts

Week 4

Loving myself is worth all of my energy and dedication. No one loves me more than I can love myself. How did you love yourself this month? Are you taking this same energy into the next month?

For Your Thoughts

Spring renewal

March

Week 1

Set your intentions for the week... What are you choosing this week? Love, anger, forgiveness, grace, or patience? All of these can exist this week, but let's decide how we exhibit these different emotions.

For Your Thoughts

Week 2

Start this week with gratitude. What are you thankful for? Gratitude has no limit - Be grateful for your beauty, be thankful for the love you have in your life, be grateful for the stranger at the store who gave you a moment of kindness with their smile.

For Your Thoughts

Week 3

Spring is in full bloom! Let's plant! Spring is the time to plant the seeds of our lives. What do you aspire to do in your life? How can you start to plant the seeds? You got this girl... no more waiting to do the things your heart and mind desires! Let's grow together!

For Your Thoughts

Week 4

You did it!! Another month has come to an end! Let's reflect: what are the good things that happened this month? Did your black/brown girl magic shine all 31 days? Girl you did soooo well this month, no matter what challenge you had, you overcame it. Loving yourself is continuing to yield high rewards. I am thankful for you loving yourself this month.

For Your Thoughts

Rebirth "Each night, when I go to sleep, I die. And the next morning, when I wake up, I am reborn."

—Mahatma Gandhi

Week 1

"Every day is a new day to start anew." "No one can stop you, but you." Set this week's intention to step out of your comfort zone. Each day you have a chance to be the person you are striving to be. No one can stop you but you. This week you will not stand in your way. GET OUT THE WAY! MOVE!

For Your Thoughts

Week 2

What do you want for your life? Spend this week examining how you are living your life and if it is the way you want. Is there anything you need to shed to begin your journey to the best you? This month is about rebirth- growing into the woman you want to become. We planted seeds last month, so continue nurturing your seeds to see what you are growing.

For Your Thoughts

Week 3

Planting seeds, growing, replanting. How do you feel this week? Does anything need to be replanted? If things need to be replanted, give yourself grace! Remember every day is a new day to start anew. This week is about Grace! How much grace have you shown yourself? How much grace are you willing to give yourself? Be gentle with yourself this week.

For Your Thoughts

Week 4

Name mantras- This week say your first name and middle name and follow it with I am... Insert the things that you desire yourself. Example :I am Ashley Andrea and I am loved, adored, and blessed to bless others.

For Your Thoughts

Week 5

Hey girl! We did it again! Another month down. Hug yourself and tell yourself how proud you are of all the accomplishments you made this month. This month you continued your growth into the wonderful black/brown woman that you are! If no one else tells you this week, know that I love you!

For Your Thoughts

Flowers: Last month we started to see the growth of the seeds we planted in March.

Week 1

You are the most beautiful flower in a sea of dandelions. Your beauty stands out no matter what distractions surround you. Spread your petals this week and allow those who need it to feed on your pollen to create more flowers around you. This simple act of kindness has rewards far beyond what you can imagine. Put good out this week, do good deeds and you will get it back tenfold.

For Your Thoughts

Week 2

What flowers are you going to nurture this week? Co-workers, friends, family, significant other? The relationship in our lives all represents different flowers. You are a flower, and to keep yourself bright and beautiful, you must also provide love to the flowers that have helped nurture you. This week let's focus on the beauty of those who continue to water our flower.

For Your Thoughts

Week 3

Take some time at the start of each day this week and sit with yourself. What are the first thoughts that come to mind? Do you feel a sense of peace? Do you feel anxious? Do you feel ready for the day? Let's practice mindfulness this week. This simply means taking few minutes each morning to examine how you are feeling before running out into the world. At the end of your moment, take a deep breath and say your first and middle name and then say, "love and light surround me today and everyone I encounter." Now take another deep breath again and exhale.

For Your Thoughts

Week 4

Girl, you are killing it once again! Another month comes to an end! Who is this beautiful, intelligent, kick-ass woman who loves herself sooooo much these first five months of the year? Oh girl, it's you! This last week is a check-in for love and abundance. What did the universe provide abundantly for May? Once you realize it, take a moment each day to express gratitude for the abundance you are experiencing.

For Your Thoughts

Summer, Summer, Summer Time- Will Smith

June

Week 1

Summer has arrived. How do you feel? Do you love the skin you are in? Tell yourself each day one thing that you love about yourself.

For Your Thoughts

Week 2

Things are in full bloom this time of year. This week allow yourself to step into the kind of woman you want to become. We cannot be the women we aspire to be if we do not start to step into the heels, ones, Jordans, slides, or sandals of who we want to be. Let's walk the walk.

For Your Thoughts

Week 3

Check in- We are midway through the year. How is it going? No regrets allowed! Anything that you did not accomplish or were disappointed by does not matter now. Let's move in the space of gratitude for the place we are in and continue to move forward.

For Your Thoughts

Week 4

It's the end of the month. Are you ready for the next month? This week let's focus on our purpose. What has the universe called you to do in this life? What does living in your purpose look like this week? Each day do something related to your purpose.

For Your Thoughts

Take It all off!

Week 1

We are in the heat of summer. Is it a hot girl summer, as Meg the Stallion says? What does the summer represent to you? It is hot in many parts of the world; what are you taking off to stay cool? Every day this week, release something that has been bothering you! We are taking it all off this summer. This week you will say, "I am infinite and have an abundance of all things seen and unseen."

For Your Thoughts

Week 2

"I am a light that shines for others, but also myself. Nothing is unattainable; all things are possible."

For Your Thoughts

Week 3

"The feds is watching." This week we are focused on accountability. What does accountability look like? What have you been holding yourself accountable to this summer? "I am accountable in all that I do!"

For Your Thoughts

Week 4

What things have brought you joy this month? Did you remove the things that didn't? "I deserve all things that enhance and enlighten my life.'

For Your Thoughts

Week 5

The end of July is here! How are we moving this week? Let's choose to move with love and positivity. Every day this week say these two statements to yourself- "I choose to operate at my highest self this week." "I choose to communicate with the highest vibration of love this week."

For Your Thoughts

"August makes me think about family! Family reunions, class reunions, friends' reunions! We are ending the summer. Have you connected with your friends and family this summer? August is about relationships and how we are operating in them and outside of them".

August

Week 1

I manifest closer ties with those who support me and ensure our bond is wrapped in love and support.

For Your Thoughts

Week 2

I am manifesting more love than fear each day this week.

For Your Thoughts

Week 3

I manifest patience for the things I do not understand or have control over in all my relationships.

For Your Thoughts

Week 4

We are in the last week of August! Ask yourself how the summer was? This week focus on the things you want to fall back from going into Fall. I am worthy of having all the desires of my heart, and I have the courage to let go of things that interfere with my desires.

For Your Thoughts

Falling back!

September

Week 1

This week, take time each morning and each evening to say, "I choose to fall back and let the universe operate on my behalf."

For Your Thoughts

Week 2

Spend some time in nature this week. Commit to spending at least 10-15 minutes outside. While outside, take 3-5 deep breathes. On the exhale, say to yourself, "I choose to live my life with ease."

For Your Thoughts

Week 3

Is there anything in your life right now that you need to fall back on? If there is, let's set the intention this week to not hold on to anything that takes away from our happiness.

For Your Thoughts

Week 4

Name mantra – "I am (insert first name and middle name) and nothing can stop my desire to live freely and peacefully."

For Your Thoughts

Week 5

You did it!! We made it to the end of another month. This week we set the intention not to be a victim of our triggers. Remember, Fall is about falling back from the things that do not serve us. Our triggers tend to keep us stuck. When you are triggered, take a moment to recognize the trigger and say, "I choose to live in the present and not be a victim of my past."

For Your Thoughts

All around the world, people are celebrating independence days and revolutions this month. This month is all about the ancestors!

October

Week 1

I am aligned with the divine. Thank you ancestors, for laying the path to my success.

For Your Thoughts

Week 2

Take time each morning and reflect on the things you have learned or gained from your ancestors. Take what you have learned or gained and apply it each day this week. We define ancestors as those who came before us, so a grandmother, aunt, or anyone who has passed away in your lifetime who played an intricate role in your life. You are a Queen!

For Your Thoughts

Week 3

Create an altar to honor those before you. The alter could have pics, their names written on a sticky note, any of their personal belongings, and anything else that you feel represents them. Each day this week and every week thereafter, take 10 minutes every day (day or night) to pray or honor them. Do not be afraid to ask your ancestors for the things you need.

For Your Thoughts

Week 4

How do you talk to yourself? Would your ancestors speak to you that way? What are the kind things your ancestors have said to you? These are the kind things you need to say to yourself every day.

For Your Thoughts

Giving Thanks

November

Week 1

I am grateful for financial abundance.

For Your Thoughts

Week 2

I am grateful for an abundance of good health and continued good health.

For Your Thoughts

Week 3

I am grateful for the abundance of love in my life.

For Your Thoughts

Week 4

We did it again! Another month down. I have given you some examples of what to be grateful for this month, so this last week tell yourself what you are grateful for!! Be intentional and say it each day this week. You can write the things you are grateful for or say them aloud.

For Your Thoughts

Full Circle- We made it to the end of the year.
December is a time to reflect on the year.

Week 1

What did you accomplish this year? What obstacles, if any, did you overcome? Take time each day this week to reflect on the year.

For Your Thoughts

Week 2

I am grateful for the challenges and the wins I have had all year. Thank you universe, for your divine intervention all year.

For Your Thoughts

Week 3

How have you loved yourself this year? How can you improve or strengthen your love for yourself? Do you love yourself enough to commit to treating yourself better? Take time each day this week to evaluate your self-love.

For Your Thoughts

Week 4

"The love I have for myself is divine, kind, and everlasting."

For Your Thoughts

Week 5

The end of the year is here. How are we going into the new year? Every day this week, say this mantra: "I am worthy of the blessings from others, I am worthy of love, I am worthy of success, I am the woman that I want to be unapologetically.

For Your Thoughts

www.ingramcontent.com/pod-product-compliance
Lightning Source LLC
Chambersburg PA
CBHW081126300726
48982CB00005B/856

* 9 7 8 1 6 3 6 1 6 0 9 0 0 *